Copyright © 2025 by Jack Tindle

ISBN: 978-1-967257-05-8 First Metric Edition, Hard Back
ISBN: 979-8-218-41187-9 First U.S. Edition, Hardback
ISBN: 979-8-218-41187-9 Ebook U.S. Edition

All rights reserved.

No portion of this book may be reproduced in any form without written permission from the publisher or author, except as permitted by U.S. copyright law.

Book design by Branch and Willow Design Co.

1st Metric Edition 2025

Edit by Jon Allen

Library of Congress Control Number: 2025945369

JAC Press, Alliance OH USA.

For permissions or inquiries, please contact
hello@booksbyjac.com

Thank you to my parents and grandparents for encouraging my mocktail-making journey in countless ways.

Thank you to my broken hand... what a blessing in disguise. *(Check out the full story online.)*

Thank you to my TikTok and Instagram communities. You all are absolutely THE BEST! I appreciate your continued support, encouragement, and sense of humor.

Thank you to my friends for encouraging me along the way and making this dream feel possible.

Table of Contents

NECESSARY BAR ITEMS AND TERMINOLOGY

1	Tools You Need
2	Tools That Are Nice to Have
3 - 4	Glassware
12	Terminology
13	Drink-Rating Levels

NON-ALCOHOLIC MOCKTAILS - EASY LEVEL

1 - 2	Cherry Sour		17 - 18	Mexican Mule
3 - 4	Piña Colada		19 - 20	Appletini
5 - 6	Dark and Stormy		21 - 22	Cherry Cheesecake
7 - 8	Peach Bellini		23 - 24	Blue Hawaii
9 - 10	Malibu Bay Breeze		25 - 26	Mint Jade
11 - 12	Raspberry Fizz		27 - 28	Daiquiri
13 - 14	Orange Creamsicle		29 - 30	Old-Fashioned
15 - 16	Mimosa		31 - 32	Margarita

Table of Contents

NON-ALCOHOLIC MOCKTAILS - INTERMEDIATE LEVEL

Pages	Recipe	Pages	Recipe
33 - 34	Grasshopper	53 - 54	Bees Knees
35 - 36	Caramel Apple	55 - 56	Toasted Marshmallow
37 - 38	Dracula's Delight	57 - 58	Apple Spice
39 - 40	Pink Honey Martini	59 - 60	Malibu Sunset
41 - 42	French 75	61 - 62	Whiskey Sour
43 - 44	Cosmopolitan	63 - 64	Nitro Pepsi Milkshake
45 - 46	Toasted Almond	65 - 66	Mai Tai
47 - 48	Mudslide	67 - 68	Agave Punch No. 2
49 - 50	Dirty Martini	69 - 70	Passionate Orange
51 - 52	B-52	71 - 72	A Passionate Kiss on the Sand

NON-ALCOHOLIC MOCKTAILS - EXPERT LEVEL

Pages	Recipe	Pages	Recipe
73 - 74	Brandy Alexander	83 - 84	Irish Milkshake
75 - 76	Smoked Old-Fashioned	85 - 86	Amaretto Sour
77 - 78	Passion Fruit Martini	87 - 88	Brown Derby
79 - 80	Ramos Gin Fizz	89 - 90	Enzoni
81 - 82	Nutty Eggnog	91 - 92	Blackberry Bramble

Tools You Will Need

Jigger
This is what you will use to measure your ingredients. It comes in a 1 and 2 oz size.

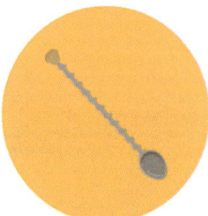

Bar Spoon
You will use this to stir your drinks and it helps with garnishing.

Shaker Tins
You will use this to shake or stir your ingredients.

Bottle Opener
You will use this to open bottles, and some have built in zesters.

Drink Strainer
Used to strain your drinks after shaking or stirring to keep the ice out.

Tools That Are Nice to Have

Pouring Spouts
This will make pouring (especially free pouring) much easier.

Blender
Many drinks, such as a piña colada, are blended in a blender with ice.

Muddler
Helps to squish things like mint or fresh fruits in the bottom of your glass or tin.

Fruit Juicer
Helps juice fresh fruits, which always makes your drinks a little better tasting.

Handheld Torch
Used to smoke drinks with wood chips, and can also be used for crème-brulee.

Glassware

Collins/Highball Glass

This is often considered the original cocktail glass and can be used in a variety of drinks.

Rocks Glass

Like the Collins glass, the rocks glass is very versatile and is a must have in my opinion.

Coupe Glass

This is typically used with sweeter gin drinks, but is fairly versatile. It was also rumored to be originally modeled after a particular part of the female anatomy...

Martini Glass

Despite its name, this glass can be used in a variety of different drinks, not just martinis.

Glassware

Hurricane Glass

This is the perfect glass for all your tropical drinks, and is named after one of them!

Margarita Glass

Although this glass is only used for margaritas, there's tons of variations for you to try!

Irish Coffee Mug

This unique mug is good for milkshakes and coffee-inspired drinks, and is one of my personal favorites.

Flute Glass

This is a beautiful glass that's perfect for drinks that use non-alcoholic champagne such as a mimosa or bellini.

Drink-Making Terminology

"Muddle"

To squish herbs or fruit with a muddler, which can be found on the tools list.

"Strain"

You will do this after shaking or stirring a drink. You'll use a strainer which you put over your shaker when you pour to avoid ice getting in the final drink.

"Chilling a Glass"

This refers to chilling a glass either with ice or leaving it in a freezer so it's cold and frosted when you pour your drink into it.

"Top/Float"

Topping with something typically means adding it after shaking the drink, usually because it's carbonated. Floating refers to "floating" a layer of liquid on top of your drink with a bar spoon or just free pouring it.

"N/A"

This isn't really common terminology but it is what I'll be using interchangeably with the phrase "non-alcoholic" throughout this book.

Drink Criteria Levels

"Easy"

These drinks will have few ingredients and typically just involve blending, shaking, or stirring your mocktail. The ingredients will also be easy to find and relatively inexpensive.

"Intermediate"

These are a bit more difficult to make. Nothing too crazy but it will take a little more time. The ingredients will also be more specialized with things such as non-alcoholic spirits that might be a tad more challenging to find. Great excuse for a road trip!

"Expert"

Almost all these mocktails use non-alcoholic spirits and have a more robust ingredients list. They also involve some complex methods such as smoking, muddling, and layering. They're super fun mocktails, just be warned, they're not for the faint of heart.

Today we will be making an...

EASY LEVEL MOCKTAIL

CHERRY SOUR
NON-ALCOHOLIC

I've got a secret recipe that's been the life of every party I've hosted! It's a breeze to whip up, with ingredients that won't break the bank. It boasts wonderfully sweet flavors and a nice fizz to add that extra little bit of kick. Best of all, it's a crowd-pleaser that'll have everyone slurping and sipping with joy! Now, some of you may have seen the half-iced glass trick, and as much as I'd like to take credit for its design, it is simply a mold that goes in the glass.

So, next time you're having friends over or hosting a party, make sure to whip one of these up, it'll be a guaranteed hit. And if you're fortunate enough to get your hands on some cranberry Sprite, it brings this mocktail to the next level!

RECIPE
SINGLE SERVING

DIRECTIONS:

- Add all ingredients EXCEPT Sprite into your shaker with a handful of ice.
- Shake vigorously for 30 seconds.
- Strain into your rocks glass using a drink strainer.
- Top with Sprite and give it a final stir.
- Take a sip of your sweet mocktail and enjoy!

INGREDIENTS:

- 30 ml Maraschino cherry syrup
- 15 ml grenadine
- 23 ml sweet and sour
- Top with Sprite. *(TIP: From past experience, don't ever put a carbonated beverage in your shaker. Very messy!)*

ROCKS GLASS

PINA COLADA
NON-ALCOHOLIC

Behold, the king of all tropical drinks, the piña colada! A sweet and savory sensation, blending together two of the best flavors in the world: coconut and pineapple. Now, there are lots of fancy ways to mix this drink, but let's stick to the classic recipe, shall we? And trust me, it's way better than those pre-made mixers you'll find at the store. Whether you're sipping your piña colada at a beachside bar, in the comfort of your own home, or even out in the snow (yes, I've done that), this drink is sure to transport you to a warm sunny paradise.

So go ahead, mix up a batch, and let the piña colada take you on a delicious journey!

Brrr... sipping a piña colada in the Michigan snow.

RECIPE
SINGLE SERVING

DIRECTIONS:

- Add all ingredients into a blender with ice.
- Blend for 1-2 minutes.
- Pour into your hurricane glass.
- Garnish with cherry or pineapple.
- Add a straw and your garnish on top.
- Sip and pair this tropical classic with some island music and your favorite island wear.

INGREDIENTS:

- 118 ml pineapple juice
- 74 ml cream of coconut
- 1 US Cup(240g/236ml) of crushed ice
- Optional 30 ml N/A light rum
- Garnish: cherry or pineapple

DARK & STORMY
NON-ALCOHOLIC

This is another one of those mocktails that surprised me. I'm not a huge fan of ginger beer, but my choice of Gosling's for this drink is probably why it was so good. Obviously, choose your own ginger beer, but for me, Goslings is my go-to.

Lyre's non-alcoholic dark rum also stands out in this drink. That said, you can omit it if you like.

This drinks not insanely complicated, but it's an easy, fun mocktail for people who enjoy a ginger-packed sweet drink.

RECIPE
SINGLE SERVING

DIRECTIONS:

- Add all ingredients EXCEPT garnish and ginger beer into your Collins glass with ice.
- Stir for about 30 seconds.
- Top with ginger beer.
- Add your garnish on top.
- Enjoy this exquisite ginger mocktail!

INGREDIENTS:

- 59 ml N/A dark rum
- 30 ml sweetened lime juice
- 119 ml ginger beer
- Garnish: lime slice

PEACH BELLINI
NON-ALCOHOLIC

When it comes to sweet fruits, peaches take the crown in my humble opinion. They're wonderfully sweet, yet sour, and this drink plays on both those notes beautifully. It's a very simple mocktail with easy ingredients... if you decide to opt for the non-alcoholic sparkling wine instead of the more difficult-to-find non-alcoholic champagne.

No matter how you make it, as long as you have some peach puree and something fizzy, this mocktail's guaranteed to give you one heck of a tasteful time!

RECIPE
SINGLE SERVING

DIRECTIONS:

- Add all ingredients into your flute glass.
- Add your garnish on top.
- Enjoy sipping on this sparkly peach mocktail that packs a peachy punch!

INGREDIENTS:

- 30 ml peach puree
- 30 ml peach syrup
- 89 ml N/A champagne or sparkling white wine
- Garnish: peach slice

MALIBU BAY BREEZE
NON-ALCOHOLIC

This drink is a total classic with a tropical twist, starring Malibu's coconut rum. However, the non-alcoholic version needed a little remix. Originally, I rocked this drink with coconut soda and it was a hit, but tracking down that delicious soda proved to be tricky.

So, I jazzed up the recipe with a mix of non-alcoholic white rum and some cream of coconut goodness. Voilà! a non-alcoholic Malibu Bay Breeze that's as refreshing as a dip in the ocean.

Whip this up on a sunny day and imagine you're on a beach vacation, mocktail in hand!

RECIPE
SINGLE SERVING

DIRECTIONS:

- Add all ingredients EXCEPT garnish into your shaker with a handful of ice.
- Shake vigorously for 30 seconds.
- Strain into your martini glass using a drink strainer.
- Add your garnish on top.
- Don't forget to add a festive paper umbrella. Now your drink is beach vacation ready!

INGREDIENTS:

- 59 ml pineapple juice
- 15 ml cranberry juice
- 15 ml cream of coconut
- 15 ml N/A white rum
- Garnish: pineapple leaves, a slice of pineapple, and a fun paper umbrella

HURRICANE GLASS

RASPBERRY FIZZ
NON-ALCOHOLIC

Raspberries, similarly to blackberries, are often underused in drinks. This has a lot to do with their tart notes, but this mocktail utilizes them perfectly. It's my own creation. and is a perfect sweet-and-sour combo.

This drink was my solution to a lack of non-alcoholic Valentine-themed mocktails, and boy, am I glad I thought of it. It also uses a tasteless powder called Luster Dust to give it the beautiful appearance depicted on the right.

So, next time you have some fresh raspberries lying around, prepare one of these delicious mocktails.

RECIPE
SINGLE SERVING

DIRECTIONS:

- Add your raspberries in your shaker and muddle them.
- Add all other ingredients EXCEPT garnish into your shaker with a handful of ice.
- Shake vigorously for 30 seconds.
- Strain into your flute glass using a drink strainer.
- Add your sparkling raspberry and garnish on top.
- Sprinkle in a bit of Luster Dust.
- Admire and sip away!

INGREDIENTS:

- 4 fresh raspberries
- 30 ml grenadine
- 59 ml cranberry cocktail
- 15 ml simple syrup
- 59 ml sparkling raspberry
- Garnish: raspberry

ORANGE CREAMSICLE
NON-ALCOHOLIC

This drink is a one-way ticket to memory lane, whisking me back to lazy summer afternoons and the joy of savoring a delightfully refreshing Creamsicle. Shockingly, this mocktail outshines the original treat, with even sweeter flavors! Crafted from my own, now not-so-secret recipe, even my mom, whose not the biggest fan of a Creamsicle, couldn't resist this drinks wonderfully sweet orange charm.

The best part about this drink is it doesn't require blending or any fancy ingredients, which makes it easy to whip up for any occasion.

RECIPE
SINGLE SERVING

DIRECTIONS:

- Add all ingredients EXCEPT garnish into your shaker with a handful of ice.
- Shake vigorously for 30 seconds.
- Strain into your rocks glass using a drink strainer.
- Add your garnish on top. *(I highly recommend adding in the Creamsicle.)*
- Relax in a cozy chair outdoors and savor!

INGREDIENTS:

- 30 ml vanilla syrup
- 15 ml N/A triple sec
- 59 ml orange juice
- 30 ml heavy cream
- 15 ml whipped cream
- Garnish: orange slice and a Creamsicle

ROCKS GLASS

MIMOSA
NON-ALCOHOLIC

Ah yes, the drink of choice for moms everywhere! The mimosa is a classic that needs no introduction, but this alcohol-free version adds a whole new burst of flavor to the party.

Of course, you could always just mix some orange juice with Sprite, but where's the fun in that? This version uses a plethora of ingredients that make for a deliciously complex and zesty orange treat.

Cheers to a new twist on an classic favorite that'll be sure to spice up any eggs and toast breakfast or brunch!

RECIPE
SINGLE SERVING

DIRECTIONS:

- Add all ingredients (champagne last) into your pre-chilled flute glass.
- Stir gently for approximately 15 seconds.
- Add your garnish on top.
- Cheers to your fun new morning treat!

INGREDIENTS:

- 44 ml orange juice
- 59 ml N/A champagne or N/A sparkling wine
- 1 dash of orange bitters
- 15 ml N/A triple sec
- Garnish: orange slice

FLUTE GLASS

MEXICAN MULE
NON-ALCOHOLIC

I'll say it right away... this drink is not for everyone. It's on the more spicy side between the jalapeno-infused non-alcoholic tequila and ginger beer. There are still some nice sweet notes, but if you can't stand anything spicy, odds are this isn't the mocktail for you.

All that being said, it's still a fun drink to try, especially if you want a non-alcoholic version of a Moscow Mule.

The kick from the non-alcoholic tequila and ginger beer is paired with unique flavors that are sure to get your tastebuds going.

RECIPE
SINGLE SERVING

DIRECTIONS:

- Add all ingredients EXCEPT garnish and ginger beer into your Collins glass with ice.
- Stir gently for about 30 seconds.
- Top with ginger beer.
- Add your garnish on top.
- Sip and feel the delightful spicy kick!

INGREDIENTS:

- 59 ml N/A spicy tequila (Ritual or Bonbuz)
- 15 ml agave syrup
- 30 ml sweetened lime juice
- 89 ml ginger beer
- Garnish: lime slice

APPLETINI
NON-ALCOHOLIC

Sour apple flavors have always been a hit in the candy world. This drink is like a sip straight out of a Laffy Taffy, bursting with that familiar sour apple tang. It's a love-it-or-leave-it kind of mocktail, packing a punch of sourness. But hey, it's a breeze to whip up and a hit with the younger crowd.

So, if you and your pals dig sour candies, this lip-puckering mocktail is absolutely a must-try!

RECIPE
SINGLE SERVING

DIRECTIONS:

- Add all ingredients EXCEPT garnish into your shaker with a handful of ice.
- Shake vigorously for 30 seconds.
- Strain into your martini glass using a drink strainer.
- Add your garnish on top.
- Time to sip away! *(Does this count for an apple a day keeps the doctor away?)*

INGREDIENTS:

- 44 ml sour apple (Cal Premium)
- 44 ml apple juice
- 15 ml sweet and sour
- Garnish: green apple slice

MARTINI GLASS

CHERRY CHEESECAKE
NON-ALCOHOLIC

I adore a scrumptious cherry cheesecake, and this mocktail is a dead-ringer for it! Believe it or not, it's not packed with cherry syrup, but rather a delightful mix of cranberry-esque flavors blended with vanilla for that cheesecake flavor. It's typically served as a shot, but I prefer to sip and relish every drop. It's a party favorite of mine, but fair warning: it's sweet like candy, so don't go overboard on this tempting treat or you'll be sorry the next day.

Paired with crushed Pop Rocks on the rim, this delicious drink might be a little too sweet for some, but perfect for others.

RECIPE
SINGLE SERVING

DIRECTIONS:

- Add all ingredients EXCEPT garnish into your shaker with a handful of ice.
- Shake vigorously for 30 seconds.
- Strain into your martini glass using a drink strainer.
- Optional: Rim with Pop Rocks.
- Have a poppin' good time enjoying your creation!

INGREDIENTS:

- 15 ml vanilla syrup
- 30 ml cranberry juice
- 15 ml grenadine
- 15 ml Luxardo cherry syrup
- Garnish: Pop Rocks (*TIP: I rimmed my glass with some cream cheese to get the Pop Rocks to stick... delicious!*)

MARTINI GLASS

BLUE HAWAII
NON-ALCOHOLIC

For all you drink connoisseurs out there, you might be expecting a blue-colored non-alcoholic piña colada, which would be the Blue Hawaiian, but hold onto your pineapples! This is something a little different. Introducing the Blue Hawaii - a tangy twist on the classic piña colada! This recipe ditches the cream of coconut and adds a dash of non-alcoholic blue curacao and sweet and sour to give it a tart kick that'll make your lips pucker!

It's perfect for anyone who's tried a piña colada and wanted it more sour and less sweet.

So, slice up your fresh pineapples, grab your tiny paper umbrella, and enjoy this Hawaiian adventure in a glass!

RECIPE
SINGLE SERVING

DIRECTIONS:

- Add all ingredients EXCEPT garnish into your shaker with a handful of ice.
- Shake vigorously for 30 seconds.
- Strain into your hurricane glass using a drink strainer.
- Add your fancy garnishes.
- Admire your gorgeous blue concoction and sip away!

INGREDIENTS:

- 89 ml pineapple juice
- 22 ml N/A blue curacao (Cal Premium)
- 30 ml sweet and sour mix
- OPTIONAL 30 ml N/A light rum
- Garnish: pineapple chunk, and of course, a fun tiny paper umbrella

MINT JADE
NON-ALCOHOLIC

Say hello to this sophisticated mocktail that's as complex as calculus (it pains me to even mention it). Sweet, sour, and minty flavors do a tango, giving your taste buds their own party. It's not just the taste that's a masterpiece, but also the eye-catching color. This drink is perfect for those who want a refreshing drink without having to use mint leaves, like you would in a mojito.

The best part? With just a handful of ingredients, you can whip up this refreshing drink in a jiffy! You only need three or four ingredients (depending on your access to N/A light rum). After a grueling day of yard work, this drink is like a cold shower for your taste buds, so enjoy!

RECIPE
SINGLE SERVING

DIRECTIONS:

- Add all ingredients into your shaker with a handful of ice.
- Shake vigorously for 30 seconds.
- Strain into your rocks or martini glass using a drink strainer.
- If pouring into a rocks glass, add a large ice cube.
- It's minty fresh green mocktail time! Enjoy!

INGREDIENTS:

- 22 ml creme de menthe
- 22 ml N/A triple sec
- 22 ml lime juice
- (OPTIONAL) 30 ml N/A light rum
- Garnish: lime slice

ROCKS OR MARTINI GLASS

DAQUIRI
NON-ALCOHOLIC

When you hear "daiquiri," what springs to mind? Probably fruity slushies you can find at just about every resort. But hold on to your cocktail shaker because this is the OG daiquiri, and it's not just a fruity mix. Instead, it's a tantalizing mix of tangy sourness and sweet sugary goodness, with a slight spicy kick from the non-alcoholic rum.

So, if you're hankering for a sweet yet complex drink that'll mix things up (pun intended), give this classic masterpiece a try.

RECIPE
SINGLE SERVING

DIRECTIONS:

- Add all ingredients EXCEPT garnish into your shaker with a handful of ice.
- Shake vigorously for 30 seconds.
- Rim glass with sugar (Makes a huge difference).
- Strain into your martini glass using a drink strainer.
- Add your garnish on top.
- Time to toast classic complex mocktails!

INGREDIENTS:

- 44 ml N/A light rum
- 30 ml lime juice
- 30 ml simple syrup
- Garnish: lemon twist or slice

MARTINI GLASS

OLD-FASHIONED
NON-ALCOHOLIC

Behold the granddaddy of all mocktails: the Old-Fashioned! It's timeless, iconic, and a true icon of pure coolness. Get ready for my all-time favorite variation with a blend of ingredients that I've spent years perfecting. This drink is not for the timid. We're talking about a drink for those who savor every second of life. It harnesses the art of subtlety masterfully, with no single ingredient stealing the show but rather all working together.

Don't hesitate! Give it a whirl, and prepare for the flavor ride of your life! And if you're looking for something even more complex, check out the smoked version of this recipe also featured in the expert section.

RECIPE
SINGLE SERVING

DIRECTIONS:

- Add all ingredients EXCEPT garnish into your mixing glass with ice.
- Stir gently for 30 seconds.
- Strain into your rocks glass with a large ice sphere or cube in it.
- Squeeze a bit of zest from an orange peel over the top of your drink and drop in the orange twist.
- Boom... you're ready to enjoy your classy mocktail!

INGREDIENTS:

- 44 ml N/A bourbon
- 15 ml honey syrup
- Fee Brothers old fashioned bitters
- Garnish: orange zest and orange twist

ROCKS GLASS

MARGARITA
NON-ALCOHOLIC

Ah yes, arguably the most infamous cocktail of all time, and for a good reason. This is a truly wonderful combination of flavors. The mix of tart from the lime and sweet from the agave and the non-alcoholic triple sec are a simple but highly effective combination. You can also add salt on the rim of your glass if you choose, but personally, it messes up the flavors for me.

This classic mocktail is perfect for all ages, and a true joy to sip on a hot sunny day.

RECIPE
SINGLE SERVING

DIRECTIONS:

- Add all ingredients EXCEPT garnish into your shaker with a handful of ice.
- Shake vigorously for 30 seconds.
- Rim your glass with salt.
- Strain into your margarita glass using a drink strainer.
- Add your garnish on top.
- Time to savor your sweet lime mocktail.

INGREDIENTS:

- 22 ml agave syrup
- 44 ml sweetened lime juice
- 30 ml N/A triple sec
- (OPTIONAL) 30 ml N/A tequila
- Garnish: lime slice

Today we will be making an...

INTERMEDIATE LEVEL MOCKTAIL

GRASSHOPPER
NON-ALCOHOLIC

This is by far one of my favorite dessert mocktails. If you enjoy mint chocolate chip ice cream, you will fall in love with this drink. It's a perfect mixture of vanilla, mint, and chocolate.

But be warned: always be careful with your non-alcoholic crème de menthe. It is super strong, and if you add too much, your beautiful minty drink will turn into a toothpaste-like disaster. Yikes!

So with that advice, I HIGHLY recommend trying this drink at one point or another. It's a game-changer for your mocktail enjoying tastebuds!

RECIPE
SINGLE SERVING

DIRECTIONS:

- Add all ingredients EXCEPT garnish into your blender with ice.
- Blend for roughly 1 minute.
- Pour into your rocks glass.
- Add your garnish on top.
- Voila! Enjoy your sweet minty creation.

INGREDIENTS:

- 3 scoops vanilla or mint ice cream
- 15 ml N/A creme de menthe
- 15 ml peppermint syrup
- 30 ml N/A creme de cacao
- 15 ml chocolate syrup
- 3 cups (710 ml) of ice
- Garnish: cinnamon stick

ROCKS GLASS

CARAMEL APPLE
NON-ALCOHOLIC

Oh, sweet nostalgia! This mocktail is my baby and was one of the first videos on my TikTok to go viral. It's a delicious autumn delight that hits all the right notes. Yes, it's a little on the sweet side, but oh my! The warm apple notes shine through, and the cinnamon and caramel flavors are to die for. It's like a warm hug in a glass.

Next time you happen to have some apple cider in your refrigerator, definitely don't be afraid to give this nostalgic drink a try.

RECIPE
SINGLE SERVING

DIRECTIONS:

- Add all ingredients EXCEPT garnish into your shaker with a handful of ice.
- Shake vigorously for 30 seconds.
- Strain into your beer mug using a drink strainer.
- Add your garnish on top.
- Savor your delightful concoction. *(Hit me up on my social to let me know what you think of this one.)*

INGREDIENTS:

- 44 ml N/A whiskey
- 118 ml apple cider
- 15 ml cinnamon syrup
- 30 ml caramel syrup
- Garnish: apple slice

BEER MUG

DRACULA'S DELIGHT
NON-ALCOHOLIC

This drink is perfect for Halloween parties, and will definitely leave an impression. It's my own design and utilizes the delicious syrup found in Luxardo cherry containers. It has a rich cherry taste, and when paired with the more sour notes in this drink, it's wonderfully wicked. Also don't forget about the dried-out pineapple slice that appears to have had all the juice sucked out of it. I wonder what that could be a reference to?

Definitely give this one-of-a-kind mocktail a try if you're looking for a spookalicous drink for the haunting season.

RECIPE
SINGLE SERVING

DIRECTIONS:

- Add all ingredients EXCEPT garnish into your shaker with a handful of ice.
- Shake vigorously for 30 seconds.
- Strain into your coupe glass using a drink strainer.
- Add your garnish on top.
- I recommend grabbing a "bite" to eat with this one. *(I just had to throw in a Dad joke.)*

INGREDIENTS:

- 59 ml pineapple juice
- 30 ml cranberry juice
- 15 ml grenadine
- 15 ml Luxardo cherry syrup
- Garnish: dehydrated pineapple slice

PINK HONEY MARTINI
NON-ALCOHOLIC

This drink is another great option for cranberry lovers. It's like the cosmopolitan's easygoing cousin, with a touch of sparkle and honey that'll make your taste buds sing. It also adds some sweet maraschino cherries for garnish to top off this sparkling cranberry treat in a glass. For those that don't have honey syrup, you can make your own substitute by mixing honey and water together.

If you've ever wanted something a little sweeter than a non-alcoholic Cosmo, this will definitely do the trick.

RECIPE
SINGLE SERVING

DIRECTIONS:

- Add all ingredients EXCEPT sparkling cranberry and garnish into your shaker with ice.
- Shake vigorously for 30 seconds
- Strain into your martini glass using a drink strainer.
- Top with sparkling cranberry and gently stir.
- Add your garnish on top.
- Sip and admire your vibrant creation!

INGREDIENTS:

- 44 ml sparkling cranberry (Stella Rosa)
- 30 ml cranberry cocktail
- 30 ml honey syrup
- 15 ml sweet and sour
- Garnish: maraschino cherry on a fancy pick

MARTINI GLASS

FRENCH-75
NON-ALCOHOLIC

Okay, let's clear the air. This drink isn't green, the lighting just got all wacky. But don't worry, this mocktail is still the real deal. The non-alcoholic champagne and gin is truly a match made in heaven! My secret ingredient for this mocktail? Honey syrup, baby! It's like a party for your taste buds and way better than boring old simple syrup. And let's talk presentation: who doesn't feel like royalty sipping out of a champagne flute? I'm telling you, it's like a whole new level of fancy for this already luxurious mocktail.

Grab your fancy glass and enjoy this herbal, sweet, fizzy concoction!

RECIPE
SINGLE SERVING

DIRECTIONS:

- Add all ingredients EXCEPT N/A champagne into your shaker with a handful of ice.
- Shake vigorously for 30 seconds.
- Strain into your champagne flute using a drink strainer.
- Top with N/A champagne and gently stir.
- Time to sit back and enjoy your fancy mocktail.

INGREDIENTS:

- 30 ml N/A gin
- 15 ml honey syrup
- 15 ml lemon juice
- 88.72 ml N/A champagne
- Garnish: lemon twist

FLUTE GLASS

COSMOPOLITAN
NON-ALCOHOLIC

Are you a cranberry fan? Then this drink is the one for you! It's a mouthwatering mix of tangy citrus and tart cranberry that will have you asking for seconds. It's a bonus if you happen to be a fan of Sex and the City as this drink was prominently featured with Carrie and her friends drinking one pretty much every episode. The lemon or orange twist is also the classic garnish for this mocktail and adds a little extra pizazz.

Still, if you have a sweet tooth, this might be a bit too much pucker for your taste buds. Don't knock it 'til you try it, though! Give it a sip and let your taste buds do the talking!

RECIPE
SINGLE SERVING

DIRECTIONS:

- Add all ingredients EXCEPT garnish into your shaker with a handful of ice.
- Shake vigorously for 30 seconds.
- Strain into your pre-chilled martini glass using a drink strainer.
- Sip and channel your inner Carrie Bradshaw!

INGREDIENTS:

- 59 ml cranberry cocktail
- 30 ml lime juice
- 15 ml sweet and sour
- 30 ml N/A triple sec
- Garnish: lemon peel twist

TOASTED ALMOND
NON-ALCOHOLIC

This mocktail is like a unicorn in a glass - unique, magical, and oh-so-sweet! With every sip, your taste buds do a happy dance to the tune of the non-alcoholic amaretto's nutty goodness. It's like a sweet symphony of coffee, almonds, and vanilla, but the nutty almond notes take center stage in this drink. While a non-alcoholic amaretto sour showcases amaretto's more sweet bitter notes, this mocktail focuses on its sweeter, more gentle side.

Whip one of these up in the dead of winter or the heat of summer - it's a hit any time of the year!

RECIPE
SINGLE SERVING

DIRECTIONS:

- Add all ingredients EXCEPT garnish into your shaker with a handful of ice.
- Shake vigorously for 30 seconds.
- Strain into your martini glass using a drink strainer.
- Add your garnish on top.
- Enjoy your sweet nutty mocktail!

INGREDIENTS:

- 44 ml N/A amaretto
- 22 ml N/A coffee liquor (Torani or lyres)
- 30 ml heavy cream
- Garnish: grated nutmeg

MARTINI GLASS

MUDSLIDE
NON-ALCOHOLIC

Coffee is amazing by itself, but it's even better in this dessert-like mocktail. There's a ton of different ways to make this, but this version is a little less sweet.

That being said, you can substitute the heavy cream for vanilla ice cream if you have more of a sweet tooth.

I also painted the glass with some chocolate swirls and added some more chocolate sauce and sugar to the rim.

For all the coffee lovers out there, this one is definitely worth a try.

RECIPE
SINGLE SERVING

DIRECTIONS:

- Decorate your martini glass with chocolate syrup and sugar.
- Add all ingredients into your shaker with a handful of ice.
- Shake vigorously for 30 seconds.
- Strain into your martini glass using a drink strainer.
- Add your garnish on top.
- Time for a coffee mocktail break!

INGREDIENTS:

- 30 ml N/A coffee liqueur (Lyres)
- 15 ml coffee liqueur syrup (Torani)
- 15 ml Irish cream syrup (Torani)
- 44 ml heavy cream
- Garnish: chocolate sauce/sugar

MARTINI GLASS

DIRTY MARTINI
NON-ALCOHOLIC

Let's get real: this drink just doesn't do it for me, whether it's the salty olive kick or the super-dry aftertaste, it's not my cup of tea. But hey, if you're an olive addict, go ahead and give it a whirl! Made with N/A dry vermouth and gin, it's a fancy mocktail whose ingredients might break the bank if you're not a diehard fan of herb-infused drinks. As a bonus, this is the only drink in one of my videos to receive a -9/10, and even if that doesn't make sense on a scale, I still stand by it.

With all that being said, don't let this mocktail turn you away from others using non-alcoholic Gin as it can be beautifully complex given the right flavor combo. So if you're looking for something new and unique to try and you happen to have the ingredients, definitely give this a whirl.

RECIPE
SINGLE SERVING

DIRECTIONS:

- Add all ingredients EXCEPT garnish into a mixing glass with a handful of ice.
- Stir for 30 seconds. *(No shaking, we're not James Bond.)*
- Strain into your pre-chilled martini glass using a drink strainer.
- Add your garnish on top.
- Enjoy your herbal olive mocktail! Stirred not shaken.

INGREDIENTS:

- 59 ml N/A gin
- 15 ml N/A dry vermouth
- 15 ml olive brine
- Garnish: green olives

B-52
NON-ALCOHOLIC

All my coffee lovers out there listen up! This is an amazing coffee mocktail that utilizes some unique ingredients that all result in a phenomenal final drink. It's multilayered, which gives it a spectacular presentation, and adds to the unique flavor profile.

That being said, I did have to make my own non-alcoholic Irish cream. I did this by mixing half and half with Torani Irish Cream syrup.

Whether you decide to make this as a shot or a full-blown drink, you'll be wanting to whip up some more.

RECIPE
SINGLE SERVING

DIRECTIONS:

- Get creative and have fun decorating your shot glass with chocolate syrup and sugar.
- Add all ingredients into your shaker with a handful of ice.
- Shake vigorously for 30 seconds.
- Strain into your shot glass.
- Bottoms up!

INGREDIENTS:

- 30 ml N/A coffee liqueur (Lyres)
- 15 ml coffee liqueur syrup (Torani)
- 15 ml Irish cream syrup (Torani)
- 30 ml heavy cream
- Garnish: chocolate sauce/sugar rim

SHOT GLASS

BEES KNEES
NON-ALCOHOLIC

This concoction is the bee's knees... literally! It's a honey-infused drink that packs a punch thanks to its generous splash of non-alcoholic gin. Despite this, it's still very mild and palatable. Even my mom, who usually steers clear of non-alcoholic spirits, couldn't resist this drink and didn't even notice the non-alcoholic gins bite!

If you or someone else wants to try some non-alcoholic gin drinks, I would highly recommend starting with this one.

RECIPE
SINGLE SERVING

DIRECTIONS:

- Add all ingredients EXCEPT garnish into your shaker with a handful of ice.
- Shake vigorously for 30 seconds.
- Strain into your coupe glass using a drink strainer.
- Add your garnish on top.
- Enjoy your "buzz-free" drink that is full of flavor.

INGREDIENTS:

- 59 ml N/A gin
- 30 ml lemon juice
- 30 ml honey syrup
- Ganrish: lemon slice

TOASTED MARSHMALLOW
NON-ALCOHOLIC

Get ready for a mind-blowing experience with this mocktail! I've been playing around with recipes all year, but this one is a standout. It includes Monin's Toasted Marshmallow Syrup, which adds a unique and scrumptious twist to the other ingredients. The result? A sweet and complex flavor explosion that's a must-try.

And the coup de grâce? The burnt marshmallow on top for garnish!

It's easy to make, but make sure to get it perfectly toasted by using a torch or other hot flame.

RECIPE
SINGLE SERVING

DIRECTIONS:

- Add all ingredients EXCEPT garnish into your shaker with a handful of ice.
- Shake vigorously for 30 seconds.
- Strain into your martini glass using a drink strainer.
- Add your delicious toasted marshmallow garnish on the rim.
- Savor your toasty concoction!

INGREDIENTS:

- 44 ml Monin toasted marshmallow syrup
- 15 ml N/A creme de cacao
- 15 ml N/A Irish cream
- 30 ml heavy cream
- 30 ml whole milk
- Garnish: toasted marshmallow

MARTINI GLASS

SPICED APPLE
NON-ALCOHOLIC

As the leaves change to brown and apple cider flows, this mocktail is a match made in autumn heaven. It's a spicy and tangy burst of flavors that'll have you leaping into piles of crunchy leaves! Unfortunately, it's a bit of a VIP recipe since Williams Sonoma no longer makes the spiced apple mix that's the star of the show, but no worries! Cinnamon syrup will save the day as a sweet substitute with a little extra apple cider.

The next time you're planning a Fall or Halloween party, make sure to whip up a batch of these mouthwatering mocktails.

RECIPE
SINGLE SERVING

DIRECTIONS:

- Add all ingredients EXCEPT garnish into your shaker with a handful of ice.
- Shake vigorously for 30 seconds.
- Strain into your martini glass using a drink strainer.
- Add your garnish on top.
- Time to get festive with your Fall-themed mocktail!

INGREDIENTS:

- 30 ml spiced apple mix
- 30 ml N/A Spiced Rum
- 59 ml apple cider
- 15 ml lemon juice
- 3 dashes of cinnamon bitters or old-fashioned bitters
- Garnish: apple slice

MARTINI GLASS

MALIBU SUNSET
NON-ALCOHOLIC

Okay, let's be real. Pineapple and coconut combinations can be a bit repetitive with little innovation or change. But what if we added a zesty twist? Drumroll please ... enter this Orange-Pineapple-Coconut mocktail! Sweet, tangy, and tropically delicious. It's like a beach party in a glass! And let's not forget the namesake of this drink. A splash of grenadine at the bottom of the glass creates a sunset effect for that extra WOW factor.

This beauty is sure to impress your taste buds and your guests!

RECIPE
SINGLE SERVING

DIRECTIONS:

- Add all ingredients EXCEPT grenadine and garnish into your shaker with a handful of ice.
- Shake vigorously for 30 seconds.
- Strain into your Collins glass using a drink strainer.
- Float the grenadine to the bottom of the glass.
- Add your garnish on top.
- Drink and pair with a gorgeous sunset!

INGREDIENTS:

- 59 ml pineapple juice
- 59 ml orange juice
- 15 ml cream of coconut
- 15 ml grenadine
- Garnish: maraschino cherry or pineapple leaves

COLLINS GLASS

WHISKEY SOUR
NON-ALCOHOLIC

Like some of the other mocktails in this book, this one is definitely an acquired taste. That said, it was one of the first drinks I tried with non-alcoholic whiskey, and is what led me to fall in love with it.

Fair warning, it will burn your throat a bit, but it's totally worth it for the deep sour and citrus notes.

If you add the egg white it will also add a nice foamy layer on top that'll taste absolutely amazing. But if the idea of an egg grosses you out (even if you can't taste it), it's still great without it!

RECIPE
SINGLE SERVING

DIRECTIONS:

- Add all ingredients EXCEPT garnish into your shaker with a handful of ice.
- Shake vigorously for 30 seconds.
- Strain into your rocks glass using a drink strainer.
- Add your garnish on top.
- Time to feel the burn; but hey it's good!

INGREDIENTS:

- 44 ml N/A whiskey, scotch. or bourbon
- 30 ml lemon juice
- 15 ml honey syrup
- 15 ml egg white (OPTIONAL)
- Garnish: maraschino cherry or lemon slice

ROCKS GLASS

NITRO PEPSI MILKSHAKE
NON-ALCOHOLIC

A while back, I gave Nitro Pepsi a go and I saw a lot of potential. So, I decided to whip up something out of this world with it. Imagine a tantalizing blend of rich chocolate, creamy vanilla, and a dash of coffee, all dancing together in perfect harmony. Even though the fizz is gone, the vanilla flavor from the Nitro Pepsi still shines through, transforming this shake into a truly mind-blowing concoction.

Oh, and you see that sweet coaster under the glass? That's my own creation! You can snag one for yourself on my website and enjoy the perfect accessory for your next beverage adventure *(shameless plug)*!

RECIPE
SINGLE SERVING

DIRECTIONS:

- Add all ingredients EXCEPT garnish into your blender.
- Blend for roughly a minute until smooth.
- Pour into your Irish coffee glass.
- Add your garnish on top.
- Enjoy sipping on your soda-inspired milkshake!

INGREDIENTS:

- 177 ml vanilla Nitro Pepsi
- 2 scoops vanilla ice cream
- 22 ml N/A crème de cacao
- 15 ml chocolate syrup
- 22 ml N/A Kahlua
- 2 cups (473 ml) of ice
- Garnish: whipped cream and chocolate syrup

IRISH COFFEE MUG

MAI TAI
NON-ALCOHOLIC

Even though many folks assume this drink is all about pineapples, surprise! It's actually not. The original version is pineapple-free. This non-alcoholic twist is the same, and keeps the tropical vibes alive with a mix of dark and light non-alcoholic rum, zesty lime juice, and orgeat (the real star, in my opinion). Orgeat is a sweet almond syrup that's a must-have in this clever drink.

This concoction is a tropical party in a glass... perfect for whenever you crave a unique alternative to a piña colada.

Cheers to a sip of the unexpected!

RECIPE
SINGLE SERVING

DIRECTIONS:

- Add all ingredients EXCEPT garnish and N/A dark rum into your shaker with ice.
- Shake vigorously for 30 seconds.
- Strain into your rocks glass using a drink strainer.
- Float your N/A dark rum on top.
- Add your garnish on top.
- Sip and pair with relaxing island music.

INGREDIENTS:

- 30 ml N/A light rum
- 30 ml orgeat
- 22 ml sweetened lime juice
- 15 ml N/A triple sec
- 30 ml N/A dark rum (to float)
- Garnish: lime slice

ROCKS GLASS

AGAVE PUNCH NO.2
NON-ALCOHOLIC

Listen up, folks... agave is amazing! If anyone tells you otherwise, they're either fibbing or missing out on one of life's greatest pleasures. Now, let's talk mocktails. Unfortunately, most don't give agave the spotlight it deserves. Well, hold onto your hats, because this drink is about to shake things up! It's a little on the sour side, but that just makes the sweet, sweet agave flavor pop even more.

Think sweet and sour candy mixed with a refreshing glass of lemonade, but a million times better.

Trust me, you will want to make a whole bunch of these for your next gathering.

RECIPE
SINGLE SERVING

DIRECTIONS:

- Add all ingredients EXCEPT garnish into your shaker with a handful of ice.
- Shake vigorously for 30 seconds.
- Strain into your rocks glass using a drink strainer.
- Add your garnish on top.
- Hit the lounge chair and enjoy your sour masterpiece!

INGREDIENTS:

- 44 ml agave syrup
- 89 ml pineapple juice
- 30 ml sweetened lime juice
- 30 ml lemon juice
- Garnish: lemon slice

ROCKS GLASS

PASSIONATE ORANGE
NON-ALCOHOLIC

Passion fruit has some amazing flavors that go super well with a variety of other fruits and syrups. In this particular mocktail, I combined it with oranges and sweet almond syrup (orgeat). The end result is a super sweet fruit blast that has further increased my passionate love for passion fruit. I've done a lot of experimenting with orgeat which adds the sweet almond notes in this drink. I've found it goes great with oranges, which in turn go great with passion fruit.

Enjoy this sweet fruity mocktail and the beautiful color that comes along with it!

RECIPE
SINGLE SERVING

DIRECTIONS:

- Add all ingredients EXCEPT garnish into your shaker with a handful of ice.
- Shake vigorously for 30 seconds.
- Strain into your coupe glass using a drink strainer.
- Admire your fruity sweet mocktail, and of course, enjoy the tasting experience.

INGREDIENTS:

- 30 ml passion fruit purée
- 15 ml orgeat
- 44 ml orange juice
- 15 ml N/A triple sec
- Garnish: orange slice

COUPE GLASS

PASSIONATE KISS ON THE SAND
NON-ALCOHOLIC

As soon as you lay eyes on the picture below, you can't help but notice that amazing glass. Yup, it's totally made of ice, which makes this drink a real showstopper. The drink itself is one of my all-time favorites, even if I did have to change the original name for any young readers. It's a hit with everyone, from kiddos to grown-ups.

But let's get real... the ice glass is the main star of the show. If you're brave enough to give it a whirl, your friends will be super impressed. Just don't take too long to sip this bad boy as the ice glass only lasts about fifteen minutes before it starts to melt.

Go ahead and knock back this chilly mocktail and cool off in style!

RECIPE
SINGLE SERVING

DIRECTIONS:

- Add all ingredients EXCEPT grenadine into a shaker with a handful of ice.
- Vigorously shake for roughly 30 seconds.
- For the ice glass, fill a Solo cup up all the way with water and let set in your freezer for 2-3 hours.
- Strain into your awesome ice glass or a hurricane glass.
- Pair with your favorite mittens.

INGREDIENTS:

- 30 ml peach purée or syrup
- 44 ml orange juice
- 15 ml N/A triple sec
- 59 ml cranberry juice
- (Optional) 22 ml grenadine
- Garnish: maraschino cherries and tiny tropical umbrella

ICE GLASS OR HURRICANE GLASS

Today we will be making an...

EXPERT LEVEL MOCKTAIL

BRANDY ALEXANDER
NON-ALCOHOLIC

When it comes to dessert-themed mocktails, I'm a huge fan. But, let's be real, most of them are just chocolate or vanilla flavored clones. So, when I took a sip of this cherry-flavored gem, my taste buds were electrified! It's like sipping on a chocolate-covered cherry (yum!). Now, here's the inside scoop: I'd give the nutmeg on top a hard pass, as it brings a bitter vibe that clashes with the rich cherry and chocolate combo.

Also as a heads-up, I swapped the white crème de cacao for Torani's white chocolate sauce as it gives it a thicker texture, and of course is non-alcoholic.

RECIPE
SINGLE SERVING

DIRECTIONS:

- Add all ingredients EXCEPT garnish into your shaker with a handful of ice.
- Shake vigorously for 30 seconds.
- Double strain into a chilled coupe glass using a drink strainer and a fine strainer. *(You've got this!)*
- Add your garnish on top.
- Dive into your dessert-themed mocktail.

INGREDIENTS:

- 44 ml "Best Regards" N/A brandy (very good but also can't be used in much)
- 30 ml white chocolate sauce
- 30 ml heavy cream
- Garnish: grated nutmeg

COUPE GLASS

SMOKED OLD-FASHIONED
NON-ALCOHOLIC

Believe it or not, there's a way to make a lip-smacking non-alcoholic old-fashioned! Usually, non-alcoholic versions of classic spirit-heavy drinks fall flat, leaving a watery aftertaste. But wait! Here's where things get interesting. Adding smoke to the drink fills that void and brings in some savory notes. The non-alcoholic bourbon or whiskey you use is key.

Lyres is a top pick, but another solid hit is Ritual's non-alcoholic whiskey. Trust me, this mocktail is a game-changer in the realm of complex, savory drinks. It will leave you and your friends in awe.

Just remember, safety first when wielding your torch, but don't forget to have a blast!

RECIPE
SINGLE SERVING

DIRECTIONS:

- Add all liquid ingredients into a mixing glass.
- Gently stir with a small handful of ice for roughly 30 seconds.
- Strain into your rocks glass using a drink strainer.
- Put the smoking lid over the glass and add your wood chips.
- Light the woodchips with a butane torch and let set for about one minute. *(Savor the wonderful smell!)*
- Remove the lid, add your large ice cube, and orange peel zest.
- BOOM! Time to kick back and enjoy.

INGREDIENTS:

- 59 ml Lyres N/A bourbon, or your choice of N/A whiskey
- 15 ml simple syrup
- 2 dashes of aromatic or old-fashioned bitters
- Pecan or oak wood chips to smoke
- Butane torch for lighting the wood chips
- Garnish: zest from an orange peel

ROCKS GLASS

PASSION FRUIT MARTINI
NON-ALCOHOLIC

I had a bit of a moral dilemma about this one. The name of the drink originally made me raise an eyebrow, so I changed it to be a bit more kid-friendly. But man, oh man the taste was simply to die for! Have you tried passion fruit? It's like a carnival on your tastebuds, with a blend of pineapple, mango, and other fruity goodness. It also has a nice bit of sourness and a little extra fizz from the non-alcoholic sparkling wine.

Extra points if you do know the original name of this drink. But hey, you can call it whatever you want. Just make sure to give it a taste - you won't regret it!

RECIPE
SINGLE SERVING

DIRECTIONS:

- Add all ingredients EXCEPT garnish and N/A wine into your shaker with a handful of ice.
- Shake vigorously for 30 seconds.
- Strain into your pre-chilled martini glass using a drink strainer.
- Top with your sparkling wine and stir.
- Add your garnish on top.
- Enjoy sipping the fruits of your labor.

INGREDIENTS:

- 44 ml passion fruit puree
- 30 ml vanilla syrup
- 15 ml sweetened lime juice
- 59 ml N/A sparkling wine
- Garnish: dehydrated orange slice

MARTINI GLASS

RAMOS GIN FIZZ
NON-ALCOHOLIC

If you mention this drink to me, prepare for some complaining! I'll grumble about the mess, the fuss, and the hassle. But don't get me wrong, this drink is worth every bit of the trouble. It's a sweetened-up twist on the original recipe. The way it blends herbal, sour, and sweet notes creates a clean, tasty composition. Plus, it's a showstopper with that foamy head bubbling over the rim of the glass.

Just a heads up though, this drink is not for the inexperienced. It's a wild ride with a long list of ingredients that pack a serious punch!

RECIPE
SINGLE SERVING

DIRECTIONS:

- In a shaker tin add all the ingredients EXCEPT the club soda.
- Add the spring on your strainer into the tin and dry shake for 1 minute.
- Remove the spring, and add a handful of ice.
- Shake again vigorously for 1-2 minutes.
- Strain into your Collins glass and slowly top with club soda.
- This double-shaker is sure to be a hit!

INGREDIENTS:

- 59 ml Ritual N/A gin
- 15 ml lemon juice
- 15 ml lime juice
- 15 ml simple syrup
- 15 ml vanilla syrup
- 15 ml heavy cream
- 22 ml egg white or aquafaba
- Top with club soda

COLLINS GLASS

NUTTY EGGNOG
NON-ALCOHOLIC

Eggnog's one of those seasonal traditions that everyone might not love, but it always brings nostalgia and fun.

Personally, I'm a big fan of eggnog and this creative mocktail makes the already amazing beverage even better. The almond flavors from the non-alcoholic amaretto go amazing with the eggnog, plus the vanilla and cinnamon notes add a nice extra touch of sweetness.

This mocktail will have everyone wondering what magical brand of eggnog you bought, and where they can get some more!

RECIPE
SINGLE SERVING

DIRECTIONS:

- Add all ingredients EXCEPT garnish into your shaker with a handful of ice.
- Shake vigorously for 30 seconds
- Double strain into a rocks glass using a drink strainer and a fine strainer.
- Add your garnish on top.
- Enjoy your fun festive mocktail!

INGREDIENTS:

- 30 ml vanilla syrup
- 15 ml cinnamon syrup
- 30 ml N/A amaretto
- 118 ml eggnog
- Garnish: nutmeg and cinnamon stick

ROCKS GLASS

IRISH MILKSHAKE
NON-ALCOHOLIC

I'm not a huge fan of Guinness's non-alcoholic beer, which has nothing to do with the quality and everything to do with preference. But hold the phone! I've discovered the holy grail of mocktails: this non-alcoholic Irish milkshake, which uses Guiness's non-alcoholic stout. This creamy yet dreamy treat is a symphony of flavors, blending together the best of non-alcoholic Guinness's coffee taste and sweet notes.

If you're a coffee addict who also craves a good milkshake from time to time, this is a must-try marvel. And of course, it never hurts to add a little whipped cream and chocolate syrup on top for garnish.

RECIPE
SINGLE SERVING

DIRECTIONS:

- Add all ingredients EXCEPT garnish into your blender.
- Blend for roughly 1 minute until smooth.
- Pour into your beer mug.
- Add your garnish on top. *(In my opinion, there can never be too much chocolate or whipped cream!)*
- Find a cozy spot to relax and savor your delicious creation.

INGREDIENTS:

- 237 ml N/A Guinness
- 4 scoops of vanilla ice cream
- 22 ml chocolate syrup
- 44 ml N/A Irish cream
- 2 cups (473 ml) of ice
- Garnish: whipped cream and chocolate syrup

BEER MUG

AMARETTO SOUR
NON-ALCOHOLIC

As a sour drink aficionado, I'm always game for a non-alcoholic Whiskey Sour or a tangy Amaretto Sour. And boy, this non-alcoholic Amaretto Sour is a true masterpiece! The combo of apricot and almond makes this a bittersweet symphony of flavors that'll have you cheering for more. The complexity and depth of taste is truly worth every sip. The key to a great Amaretto Sour is in the balance of sweet and sour, and this recipe hits all the right notes.

Plus, it's easy to make at home with just a few simple ingredients. Whether you're hosting a party or just want to treat yourself to a delicious drink, give this non-alcoholic Amaretto Sour a try. You won't be disappointed!

RECIPE
SINGLE SERVING

DIRECTIONS:

- Add all ingredients EXCEPT garnish into your shaker with a handful of ice.
- Shake vigorously for 30 seconds.
- Strain into your rocks glass using a drink strainer.
- Add your garnish on top.
- Enjoy sipping on your tangy delight!

INGREDIENTS:

- 44 ml N/A amaretto
- 22 ml N/A bourbon
- 30 ml lemon juice
- 15 ml simple syrup
- (Optional) egg white
- Garnish: lemon peel or Luxardo cherries *(I recommend trying these cherries.. they are incredible!)*

ROCKS GLASS

BROWN DERBY
NON-ALCOHOLIC

Mocktails that nail the perfect balance between flavors are rare gems, especially ones that celebrate the glorious grapefruit. But this mocktail is a true rockstar! It's a masterful blend of flavors that'll take your taste buds on a wild ride. Let's talk about the star of the show, Fever Tree's special pink grapefruit.

Usually, I'm not a fan of overpowering herbal blends when it comes to grapefruit, but Fever Tree hits the sweet spot with this one.

With all the other phenomenal ingredients, this is a grapefruit extravaganza that leaves you wanting more!

RECIPE
SINGLE SERVING

DIRECTIONS:

- Add all ingredients EXCEPT sparkling grapefruit and garnish into your shaker with a handful of ice.
- Shake vigorously for 30 seconds.
- Strain into your coupe glass with your drink strainer.
- Top with sparkling grapefruit juice and gently stir.
- Add your garnish on top.
- Enjoy and get ready to fall in love with grapefruit.

INGREDIENTS:

- 44 ml N/A bourbon
- 30 ml Fever tree sparkling pink grapefruit juice
- 15 ml honey syrup
- Garnish: orange or grapefruit slice

COUPE GLASS

ENZONI
NON-ALCOHOLIC

Who knew a grape could transform a classic Negroni into a whole new adventure! The non-alcoholic Enzoni is like the Negroni's funky cousin who always likes to surprise you.

Instead of N/A sweet vermouth, it uses grapes! Yeah, seriously! I didn't expect it either. This gives it a whole new flavor profile. It's like a bitter grape, which might not sound like the most appealing thing, but trust me, it's worth a sip.

But don't just take my word for it, try it yourself, and let your taste buds be the judge of this zany concoction!

RECIPE
SINGLE SERVING

DIRECTIONS:

- Muddle your grapes in the bottom of your shaker tin.
- Add all other ingredients EXCEPT garnish into your shaker with a handful of ice.
- Shake vigorously for 30 seconds.
- Strain into your rocks glass using a drink strainer.
- Add your garnish on top.
- Savor your bitter-sweet mocktail creation.

INGREDIENTS:

- 3-4 green grapes
- 44 ml N/A gin
- 30 ml N/A campari
- 15 ml simple syrup
- Garnish: grapes

ROCKS GLASS

BLACKBERRY BRAMBLE
NON-ALCOHOLIC

Blackberry is a tricky fruit to include in a mocktail. The drink can end up being too syrupy sweet or bitterly sour. But this bad boy right here is the exception! It's got a killer combo of sweet and bitter, with the blackberry flavor stealing the show. It also works with Ritual's non-alcoholic gin perfectly, adding nice herbal notes without being too overpowering.

This mocktail is the perfect refreshing drink for any occasion, and its unique combination of flavors is sure to impress your guests.

RECIPE
SINGLE SERVING

DIRECTIONS:

- Muddle your blackberries in the bottom of your shaker tin.
- Add all other ingredients EXCEPT garnish into your shaker with a handful of ice.
- Shake vigorously for 30 seconds.
- Double strain into your rocks glass using a drink strainer.
- Add your garnish on top.
- Time to savor your delicious blackberry mocktail. Cheers from me to you!

INGREDIENTS:

- 44 ml N/A gin
- 30 ml lemon juice
- 30 ml blackberry syrup
- 3-4 fresh blackberries
- Garnish: blackberries

ROCKS GLASS

Hello... Jack here!
Welcome to the wonderful world of mocktail making.

Thank you so much for supporting my love of mocktail-making by purchasing my book. It means the world to me!

My goal was to make not just a basic recipe book but tell my stories and create something I'm truly proud to share. Writing this has led me to reminisce about some of the amazing experiences I had while making these drinks and filming the videos.

I've had tons of fun making these creative and tasty non-alcoholic drinks throughout the last two years. I'm excited for you to try your hand at making them... and I'm betting that once you get started, you too will get hooked on mocktails.

I challenge you to create your very own mocktail recipe. On the next page is a recipe template for you to fill out. I can't wait to see what you come up with!

Cheers from Michigan,
The Teenage Bartender

photo credit:
Natalia Mae Photography

Please join me in my mocktail-making adventures on:

TikTok:
The_Teenage_Bartender

Instagram:
@the_teenage_bartender

Shopify:
www.theteenagebartender.com

Today we will be making a...

DIRECTIONS:

INGREDIENTS:

Tag me on Instagram with your unique creation!
@the_teenage_bartender

www.ingramcontent.com/pod-product-compliance
Lightning Source LLC
Chambersburg PA
CBRC091204010526
44107CB00021B/1244